SIZZLING Celebrities

Demi!

LATINA STAR DEMI LOVATO

BY JEFF BURLINGAME

Enslow Publishers, Inc.
40 Industrial Road
Box 398
Berkeley Heights, NJ 07922
USA
http://www.enslow.com

Library of Congress Cataloging-in-Publication Data:

Burlingame, Jeff.
  Demi! : Latina star Demi Lovato / Jeff Burlingame.
     p. cm. — (Sizzling celebrities)
  Summary: "Read about Demi's early life, how she got started in acting and music, and her future plans"—Provided by publisher.
  Includes bibliographical references and index.
  Includes webliography.
  ISBN 978-0-7660-4169-1
  1. Lovato, Demi, 1992- 2. Actors—United States—Biography. 3. Singers—United States—Biography. I. Title.
  PN2287.L656B87 2013
  792.02'8092—dc23
  [B]
                        2012021675

Future editions:
Paperback ISBN: 978-1-4644-0277-7
EPUB ISBN: 978-1-4645-1175-2
Single-User PDF ISBN: 978-1-4646-1175-9
Multi-User PDF ISBN: 978-0-7660-5804-0

Printed in China

012013 Leo Paper Group, Heshan City, Guangdong, China

10 9 8 7 6 5 4 3 2 1

To Our Readers: We have done our best to make sure all Internet addresses in this book were active and appropriate when we went to press. However, the author and the publisher have no control over and assume no liability for the material available on those Internet sites or on other Web sites they may link to. Any comments or suggestions can be sent by e-mail to comments@enslow.com or to the address on the back cover.

Photo Credits: AP Photo: Charles Sykes, p. 34, Chris Pizzello, pp. 11, 27, 31, 35, 36, Dan Steinberg, p. 14, Donna McWilliam, p. 13, Evan Agostini, pp. 21, 22, 32, 38, iHeartRadio, Joel Ryan, p. 6, Katy Winn, p. 40–41, Matt Sayles, pp. 4, 45; Matt Slocum, p. 8, Reinhold Matay, p. 17, Scott Gries, p. 7; John Shearer/Invision/AP Images, p. 44; Jordan Strauss/Invision/AP, p. 46.

Cover Photo: Jordan Strauss/Invision/AP (Demi Lovato at The X Factor season finale in 2012.)

Contents

CHAPTER 1
Texas Talent, 5

CHAPTER 2
A Star Is Born, 9

CHAPTER 3
Rising Star, 17

CHAPTER 4
Hot Under the Lights, 30

CHAPTER 5
Staying Strong, 43

Further Info, 47
Index, 48

Texas Talent

Demi Lovato had many reasons to be excited. Here she was at Game 5 of the 2011 World Series, ready to sing the national anthem. Nearly 20 million Americans would be watching on TV. Viewers in more than 200 other nations would be tuning in, too. To top it off, the game was in Arlington, Texas—just thirty miles from Demi's hometown.

There were 51,000 baseball fans in the stands waiting for the crucial game to begin after Demi sang. Although she had sung in front of large crowds plenty of times, Demi was especially nervous this time. "I feel like I'm about to jump out of a plane," she told MTV before the game.

Demi was chosen to sing the anthem at such a high-profile event because her fans had started an online petition to help their nineteen-year-old idol. The petition was sent to the home team, the Texas Rangers, and also to Major League Baseball. "They saw it and they called," Lovato said. "I'm so excited I just nearly died when I found out. I cannot wait." Demi also made sure to give all the credit to her fans for helping her land the

◀ *Demi Lovato poses backstage with her award for favorite pop artist at the People's Choice Awards in January, 2012 in Los Angeles.*

◄ Demi Lovato even makes trips to visit her fans, or "Lovatics," in England. Here she is on April 3, 2012, before signing copies of her new CD Unbroken for her most devoted British fans.

prestigious singing gig. She tweeted, "Only my [fans] could land me a spot singing the national anthem at the WORLD SERIES!!!! I couldn't do it without you guys!!!!"

Over the years, Demi's die-hard fans had always stood behind her. They had gone through her many ups and downs. Many had followed her career since she was seven. Those fans then saw her land roles in major TV shows such as *Sonny with a Chance* and the *Camp Rock* movies. They helped her music albums and singles reach the top of the charts, watched her win big awards, and came in droves to her tours. That's why Demi decided to give them a fond nickname, the Lovatics.

Those same fans had also lived through Demi's personal struggles. Those struggles took her away from the limelight while she entered treatment for emotional and behavioral issues. And those fans all delighted as she worked her way through her problems and began to claw her way back to the top.

That hard work was paying off. On October 24, 2011, she was at the World Series at Rangers Ballpark in Arlington. Wearing

Demi's "Lovatics" were happy to get a seat at her MTV Special Stay Strong on March 6, 2012

◄ Demi couldn't help but pick sides when she wore a Texas Rangers shirt the day she sung the national anthem at Game 5 of the 2011 World Series. After all, Texas was her home state!

a red Texas Rangers jersey underneath a black jacket with matching black skirt and red lipstick, Demi stood on the field between home plate and the pitcher's mound and belted out the "Star-Spangled Banner." Afterward, Demi's fans lit up the Internet with messages saying how great she sounded and how proud they were of her. After Demi finished singing, she took to the stands to watch her home team win the game in dramatic, come-from-behind fashion. Hours before the end of the game, Demi had had a comeback victory of her own. Singing the national anthem at the World Series—after all she had been through—was one of the biggest wins of Demi's life.

...s born August 20, 1992, in
...Patrick and Dianna Lovato.
...r, was the couple's second child.
...r-year-old sister, Dallas, already
...ge and around the house. Dallas
...of family performers. The girls'
...wboys cheerleader, and also had
...y singer. Demi later said her
...r country legends such as Reba
...Demi also said her mom ended her
...ng a parent. She told the *Toronto*
...way to channel her dreams, but
...supportive, not pushy." Demi's
...n a band.

...with the rest of the family, which
...Texas. "Demi was the most
...old *RadarOnline* in 2010. "She
...ning but laugh and have fun all
...could be a star." Unfortunately,
...her parents divorced. Her mom
...salesman and former football

player named Eddie De La Garza. Dallas and Demi soon began calling their mom's new husband "Dad."

Little Demi tagged along to all her sister's lessons and performances. This helped the two Lovato girls grow close. The sisters would even create their own shows at home for their family. But it didn't take long for Demi to want to perform in public. Demi was five years old when she first did this. One early performance came when she was in kindergarten during a school talent show. Demi did not pick an easy song to sing. In fact, she picked one of the hardest. It was Celine Dion's song from *Titanic*, "My Heart Will Go On." Demi told the *Dallas Observer*, "I was on stage, and I actually messed up, but then it started going again, so it was good. And at that moment, when I stuck through it and stopped crying onstage, I guess that's when I realized, 'Wow, I don't hate this enough to run offstage.'"

Her mistake at the talent show did little to deter the strong-minded girl. Demi already had decided she wanted to be a singer. Her parents got her singing, acting, and modeling lessons with some of the best teachers in the area. Her vocal coach, Linda Septien, told the *Dallas Observer* that Demi began her lessons by singing songs that were too hard for her, just as she had with the Celine Dion song at the talent show. The coach said Demi was eager to learn and always fun to be around. She said, "I got a kick out of her, because she was so funny.... There are just some kids who are born entertaining." Demi also learned a lot about performing from big sister Dallas.

Demi competed in talent pageants and performed in local shows. She also went to several casting calls for modeling jobs, TV shows, commercials, and movies. She tried hard, but never got any jobs. When she was five years old, she went to a casting call for the popular children's TV show *Barney & Friends*. But she didn't get that part, either. She later said it was because she didn't yet know how to read. But Demi did not give up. The next year, now able to read, she went to another casting call for *Barney & Friends*.

Demi, a confident, gap-toothed brunette of Hispanic, Italian, and Irish descent, loved attention and making people smile. Her personality seemed to make her a perfect fit for TV. But so were many of the other 1,400 girls who attended the casting call. As they all were standing in line in the hot July sun waiting to be seen by producers, another little girl standing next to her caught Demi's eye. The other girl's name was Selena Gomez. Selena

Demi Lovato first met ▶ Selena Gomez (pictured) at the tryouts for Barney & Friends.

later told *Entertainment Weekly* she remembered that Demi "had a little bow in her hair, and she turned around and she looked at me and said, 'Do you want to color?' She laid her blue jean jacket down and we started to color."

Selena was auditioning for the first time in her life. A small Texas girl of Mexican descent, Selena was one month older than Demi. She had large brown eyes, and a great smile. Demi and Selena eventually became best friends.

Both girls received callbacks, which meant the producers wanted them to return for a second audition. The 1,400 girls had been reduced to a couple dozen. Though it may seem strange now, Demi's mom almost didn't let Demi go to the second audition. That's because it was scheduled for the same time as a big trip to Las Vegas, Nevada, that the family took each year. Demi's mom didn't think her daughter stood much of a chance at landing a role on *Barney & Friends*. She told the *Dallas Observer* she told the producers, "I don't know about this ... We audition for stuff all the time, and we haven't really gotten anything. I'm just not sure that I want her to miss that week of fun that she looks forward to every year, all year."

But the producers kept pushing, saying they really liked what they had seen in Demi. Finally, the mother left it up to her daughter to decide. It took Demi no time at all. She said she wanted to stay in Texas and audition. It turned out to be the right move. Both girls landed roles on the show. Selena got the part of Gianna. Demi got the role of Angela.

Joining a Hit Show

By the time Demi and Selena joined the cast, *Barney & Friends* had been a hit for years. Featuring a large purple dinosaur and a few smaller dinosaurs, the show was filmed in Texas and aired nationally on the Public Broadcasting Service (PBS). It was even shown in other countries. Preschoolers across the world, and many of their parents, became very familiar with the show's songs, especially the one that began with Barney singing: "I love you, you love me. We're a happy family." The show encourages kids to use their imaginations as Barney leads his friends on make-believe adventures.

Demi got her big break on the kids' show Barney & Friends.

◄ *Demi hugs her half-sister, Madison, at the premiere of* Jonas Brothers: The 3D Concert Experience *on February 24, 2009.*

Off the set, Demi maintained a normal life. She went to Glenhope Elementary School in Colleyville. Then, when Demi was nine, her family grew by one. Half-sister Madison De La Garza was born December 28, 2001, and quickly became the center of the family attention. Years later, Madison became an actress on the popular TV show *Desperate Housewives.*

Demi and Selena spent two years working together on *Barney & Friends.* But then both girls became too old for their roles and were replaced with younger actresses. That wasn't necessarily a sad thing. The girls had gained valuable experience on the show. They had learned about the acting business from the inside.

Music Calls

While Selena mostly focused on acting after her time on *Barney* was through, Demi turned her attention to music. After all, her mother was a good singer. She was, too, so it seemed like the perfect move. Demi and Dallas sang together in public quite a bit. Demi also took more lessons, learned to play a few instruments, and began writing songs. One of the first, written when she was eleven, was called "Moves Me." It's about a love interest who she believes is her true love and the one who "moves" her emotionally. She even filmed a music video for it. In the video, Demi is wearing a pink shirt and a black wristband and singing and dancing with several backup dancers. The video was later changed a bit and used on an instructional dance DVD that came out in 2004 called *Off Da Hook: F-Troop Style.*

Bullying Begins

The way Demi was treated by her peers changed dramatically in junior high school. There, kids were jealous of her career and bullied her. Years later, she told TV show host Ellen DeGeneres, "I never really understood why until looking back. I had a different lifestyle than everyone else." She also said the kids at her school made fun of her weight. "When I would ask them why [they teased me] they would just say, 'Well, you're fat.' I was bullied because I was too fat." She also told *Entertainment Weekly* she "had a hate wall in the bathroom, and everyone signed a petition that said 'We all hate Demi Lovato.'"

Demi asked her parents if she could leave public school. From that point on Demi was homeschooled. Homeschooling is common for teen actors, even those who are not bullied. It allows them to study on their own time and is better for their work schedules. Demi did well in homeschool and her grades improved dramatically. Selena was homeschooled, too, and she and Demi often studied together.

Demi didn't let her career suffer because of the mean things kids said to her. She continued to write songs and perform. She also looked for more acting roles. In 2004, Demi's mom took her and Selena to the Texas capital of Austin to attend a Disney Channel talent search. The network wanted to produce a show similar to its popular *Lizzie McGuire* program. Out of the thousands of kids in attendance, Disney picked Selena. She eventually wound up playing the title role of Stephanie "Stevie" Sanchez in the show *What's Stevie Thinking?*

Disney didn't pick Demi for anything. Her mom told the *Wall Street Journal* it was because, "Selena is an adorable looking Hispanic girl, and looks more Hispanic than Demi, and that's what they were looking for at the time." Demi was happy for her friend, but began to wonder if acting was her thing. "After hundreds of auditions and nothing, you're sitting home and wondering, 'What am I doing?'" she told the *New York Daily News.*

Back home in Colleyville, Demi continued singing and acting lessons and landed some jobs. She even became the national spokesgirl for Hit Clips, tiny cartridges with popular songs on them that people could play. It was Demi's job to help promote them.

In 2006, when she was fourteen, Demi landed a small part in an episode of *Prison Break*, a popular FOX television series. Demi's star seemed to be rising, but major stardom still wasn't hers. She didn't know it, of course, but her time was right around the corner.

Demi enjoyed all her guest-acting roles. Just as *Barney & Friends* had, they helped her build her skills and gain experience. But she still had her sights on becoming a major star. To do that, she needed to land a big role. Getting cast in a recurring role on a Disney Channel show, just as her best friend Selena Gomez had done, definitely would give her stardom.

In 2006, the Disney show *Hannah Montana*, which starred Miley Cyrus, quickly became a hit. (Selena Gomez would later become a regular cast member on the show in 2007.) Disney had the power to create superstars. Miley was just the latest. Disney had also been a major stepping stone for

It took a lot of tries before Demi Lovato could make a career with Disney. Here she is posing with Minnie Mouse. ▶

others, including Britney Spears, Christina Aguilera, and Justin Timberlake. If Demi was going to become a star, Disney seemed like the best place for her to do so.

Landing the Big Roles

Also in 2006, Demi went to another Disney talent search, and she finally won a role. She was cast as lead character Charlotte in the new show *As the Bell Rings*. However, it wasn't a traditional thirty-minute-long sitcom like most Disney shows. *As the Bell Rings* was a five-minute-long comedy short that was shown during commercial breaks between other shows. That didn't make Demi any less excited to be on the show. She told *Entertainment Weekly*, "I thought it was the coolest thing."

Landing the role also gave Demi a case of the nerves, because it was a comedy. She knew she could play serious roles well, but she wasn't sure about comedy. She said, "When I got the part, I actually cried. I thought, I'm not going to be able to do this—I'm not funny! I'm never going to be able to work for the Disney Channel, because they're based on comedy."

As the Bell Rings took place in a school hallway between classes. In each episode, Demi and her friends would meet to discuss trivial issues, such as "Why do girls go to the bathroom together?" Demi also got to sing and play guitar in one episode. Her ability to sing is what eventually helped Disney realize the star power Demi possessed. Longtime friend Selena Gomez also played a role in Demi's big break, which was about to arrive. Selena told the *Wall Street Journal*, "I was absolutely determined to get [Demi] on the Disney Channel with me [in a larger role]."

That finally happened in 2007, when Selena was filming *Wizards of Waverly Place*, a popular Disney series. Demi often could be found on the set, watching as her best friend filmed her scenes. One day, Selena called Demi out of the audience and had her sing in front of the producers. Without any preparation, Demi sang the difficult "Ain't No Other Man," by former Disney actor Christina Aguilera. "All of the [executives'] heads completely turned to her," Selena said. The Disney Channel's entertainment president, Gary Marsh, said, "We realized she needed to be a larger part of our programming."

Disney liked Demi so much that they decided to cast her in two major roles. In the summer of 2007, Demi was chosen to play the female lead in a Disney original movie called *Camp Rock*. Disney also picked her to play the main part in a new sitcom in the works called *Sonny with a Chance*.

Still only fifteen years old, Demi had been performing for ten years. She was ready for her new challenge and practical, too. She told the *New York Daily News*, "Of course, it's going to add some pressure—the pressure to not make mistakes, and try and keep a good head on your shoulders. Just don't believe the hype because if something happens, and you're not the next big thing. I love what I'm doing and if the rest comes, great."

Camp Rock Rules

Even before *Camp Rock* premiered, the "rest" had started coming for Demi. Newspapers and TV stations began featuring her. Many critics said she was in line to be the next Miley Cyrus. Demi's stepfather quit his job as a car salesman to become one of her co-managers. Everyone predicted Demi was going to be huge.

Camp Rock is a musical that has much in common with Demi's real life. In the movie, Demi plays Mitchie Torres, an aspiring musician who desperately wants to attend a summer camp called Camp Rock. But Mitchie's family can't afford to send her there. Mitchie eventually gets to go to the camp, but only after her mother takes a job as camp cook. Mitchie has to help her mom in the kitchen. One day, long-haired pop singer Shane Gray, played by Joe Jonas, overhears someone singing in the kitchen and loves what he hears. He begins a quest to find the amazing singer. Kevin and Nick Jonas are also in the movie.

The three Jonas Brothers were a well known boy band across the United States by the time they filmed *Camp Rock*. With the Jonas Brothers in the cast, it was all but guaranteed that *Camp Rock* would be a smash. The main question was how would Demi do in her first lead role?

A Record-Breaking Debut

The answer came June 20, 2008, when the TV movie premiered. Nearly 9 million people tuned in to watch it.

Demi's costars in Camp Rock were the Jonas Brothers. From the left are: Demi Lovato, Joe Jonas, Nick Jonas, and Kevin Jonas.

That made *Camp Rock* the second-highest-rated show in Disney Channel history behind the mega-hit *High School Musical 2*. Still, *Camp Rock*'s debut had even drawn more viewers than the original *High School Musical*.

Like the *High School Musical* series, *Camp Rock* wasn't just a movie. It was a national phenomenon. There were *Camp Rock* lunchboxes, dolls, books, pajamas, board games, and even a shower curtain. Demi's face was on a majority of the

Demi Lovato attends the Camp Rock premiere at the Ziegfeld Theater in New York City on June 11, 2008.

merchandise. Her voice was used for some of it, too. Demi sang on four of the songs on the *Camp Rock* soundtrack, including "This is Me," a duet with Joe Jonas that had been the final song performed in the movie.

The same month *Camp Rock* was released, *Star* magazine ran a story about Demi's relationship with her biological father, Patrick Lovato. Their relationship had been rocky for years. But, according to the story, it appeared the two finally were getting along well. Patrick Lovato told the *Star* that Demi had surprised him with a visit in New Mexico. He said they hadn't seen each other in four years, and, "I walked out of the bedroom, and there was Demi! I couldn't believe how beautiful she was. The first thing she said to me was, 'Hey, partner... I love you!' We threw our arms around each other and began to cry." Demi later told the *New York Daily News* that the reunion wasn't as rosy as her father had described. She said, "It didn't have the fairy tale ending that he portrayed."

Back to Music

By the time *Camp Rock* was released on DVD in August, Demi was a star, especially with young girls. But she didn't take much time to celebrate. Instead, she set out across the country to play music. She first toured by herself. Then, in September, she reunited with her *Camp Rock* co-stars, the Jonas Brothers, on their *Burnin' Up* tour. Demi turned sixteen years old on the tour. She celebrated by opening for the JoBros at a sold-out show in Atlanta, Georgia. During Demi's set, the audience twice sang happy birthday to her. That Thanksgiving, Demi even sang the national anthem at the Dallas Cowboys' football game.

Demi and the Jonas Brothers also performed together two months later at the *Kids' Inaugural: We Are the Future* concert in Washington, D.C., and also did some charity work for Disney's Friends for Change organization. For that, Demi, the JoBros, Miley Cyrus, and Selena Gomez all sang a song called "Send It On." Proceeds from the song went to help the environmental charity. Demi has also helped other charities throughout the years. According to the Web site Look to the Stars, she has helped the Kids Wish Network, City of Hope, the Red Cross, and several others.

One charity Demi helped with was particularly close to her heart. That was PACER's National Center for Bullying Prevention. Following her *Camp Rock* success, Demi became the group's national spokesperson. On PACER's Web site, she wrote, "I was bullied in middle school. People say sticks and stones may break your bones but names can never hurt you, but that's not true. Words can hurt. They hurt me. Things were said to me that I still haven't forgotten."

At the end of the *Burnin' Up* tour, Demi released her first album, an eleven-song pop rock effort called *Don't Forget*. Demi had written most of the songs with the Jonas Brothers, including some of them when they were there filming *Camp Rock*. Demi talked to the *Morning Call* newspaper of

Allentown, Pennsylvania, about her album. She said, "I really wanted to establish myself as a musician, not just the girl from *Camp Rock*. ... [But] I really just wasn't prepared to basically like [spit] out an entire album by myself. So I wrote it with them and they helped me."

Don't Forget's songs included popular singles "Get Back," and "Don't Forget," both of which Demi had written with the Jonas Brothers, and both sounded a lot like Jonas Brothers' songs, only with a female singing them. Demi admitted as much. She said the songs sounded "very Jonas." The week it was released on Disney's Hollywood Records, *Don't Forget* was the number two record in the United States. It has since gone gold, meaning it has sold more than 500,000 copies.

Demi said many of the lyrics on her first album were personal. She told *PopEater* that the angry song "Don't Forget" was about a past relationship. She said, "Everyone goes through the experience of falling in love, but then the other person just walks away, and goes somewhere else. I went through an experience like that and wanted to write about it. I got over it, and now a year later I don't have those feelings about that person anymore."

Dating Rumors

Rumors soon began swirling about Demi's love life. Namely, that she was dating Joe Jonas. Demi swore the two were never an item. She said she thought of all the JoBros as if they were her own brothers. She told the *Washington Post*, "I think I'm, like, the only girl in America who doesn't [have a crush on the brothers]. It's kinda weird because you're hanging out with your friends and all of a sudden there's hundreds of girls screaming at them and you're like … why?"

Aside from the fact that she considered him a real brother, Demi said there was one other reason she didn't date Joe Jonas: She was afraid of how his fans might treat her. She told *Entertainment Weekly*, "Imagine being new to Disney and your first big job is being the romantic interest of one of the biggest heartthrobs on the channel. Any girl that is a friend of the Jonas Brothers gets hate mail and is automatically suspected as a girlfriend." Demi also took to Twitter, where she told her millions of followers: "There's been a lot of rumors lately that I'm dating one of my best friends Joe. I can promise my entire career that I am not. We've NEVER dated. He's incredible, but we don't have feelings for each other in that way. I love you guys and I wouldn't lie about that."

Demi later admitted she was dating blond-haired *Hannah Montana* star Cody Linley at the time, but said they broke up due to her busy schedule. Some have even said Demi's song "Don't Forget" was written about him. Demi told *Popstar!*, "It's really weird because Cody's like the complete opposite of what I would normally be attracted to!" And what exactly is Demi normally attracted to? "I love rock stars. The bad boys, the bands," she said.

emi Lovato (right) ▶
ares a laugh
th fellow Sonny
th a Chance cast
embers Brandon
ychal Smith and
ffany Thornton
ile they were
uring.

"A Chance" for More Stardom

The second major role Disney had in mind for Demi when it cast her in the summer of 2007 was the part of Allison "Sonny" Munroe in the sitcom *Sonny with a Chance*. In it, Demi stars as a teen from Wisconsin who had moved to Los Angeles, California, to act in a television show called *So Random*. Basically, *Sonny* is a show within a show. The plot centers around Sonny's life at home and work and the struggles and joy she experiences in dealing with both. The show was very popular with teens and was the top-rated show on television for kids ages six through eleven.

While *Sonny with a Chance* was in the middle of its first season, another Disney TV movie starring Demi debuted. This one was called *Princess Protection Program*, and Demi's longtime friend Selena Gomez was her co-star. Both girls' careers had come a long way since the two last worked together as little kids in *Barney & Friends*. In *Princess Protection Program*, Demi plays Rosalinda, a princess from a small Spanish-speaking country who is taken to Louisiana for her safety after her country is threatened by an evil dictator. While in Louisiana, Princess Rosalinda changes her name to Rosie, and becomes friends with Selena's character, a tomboy named Carter Mason. The movie was a smash. More than 8 million people tuned in on June 26, 2009, to see the premiere.

New Music Time

Just as she had been when *Camp Rock* was released, Demi—who had recently earned her high school diploma—was on the road performing music when *Princess Protection Program* first aired. More specifically, she was in Boston, Massachusetts, on one of the first dates of her Summer 2009 tour. The tour was launched to support Demi's second album, *Here We Go Again*. It was a bit edgier than Demi's first album. Gone was the influence of the Jonas Brothers. In were more sensitive, soulful songwriters such as John Mayer and Scott Cutler, who had written songs for Miley Cyrus, Kelly Clarkson, Beyonce, and Katy Perry.

Demi told the *Morning Call*, "I feel like this is my album. It was great having the Jonas Brothers help me. But with this one, I sound a little bit more like what's coming from my heart. It's more me."

Those passionate songs included the title song, which was about a hot-and-cold relationship with a boy, and "Remember December," a sometimes-techno-sounding song about remembering the good times of a relationship. Though it could have simply been because she was more popular, Demi's coming-from-the-heart songs were better received than those she'd written with the JoBros. When it was released, *Here We Go Again* debuted at number one on the *Billboard* charts. It also went gold, just as her first album had done. It wasn't only her music—everything Demi touched at this point seemed as if it were turning to gold.

Hot Under the Lights

It's an unfortunate trend that occurs with many teen stars. They achieve tremendous popularity and success at young ages but aren't equipped to deal with it. Being a star isn't just about glitz and glamour. It also means growing up in the spotlight, having to deal with people calling you names, criticizing your clothes, and even making fun of your looks. Many teens eventually crash under the weight of such pressure. Some drop out of the profession. Others even get in trouble with drugs and alcohol.

Many people associated with Demi worried that something like that could happen to her. As early as age sixteen, Demi had hinted to the media that life as a star wasn't as easy or as glamorous as many believe it to be. She told the *Dallas Observer* that on the set of *Camp Rock*, "I got really sick of exhaustion. I was in my trailer sweating. Drips of sweat were just coming off me because I was so stressed. It really does affect your health—how much you work, especially being this young."

For most of 2010, it appeared as though Demi would be immune to any pitfalls and continue on her successful path. Her popular *Sonny with a Chance* TV series entered its second

Demi Lovato and Joe Jonas eventually confirmed that they were dating. Here they are arriving at the Kids' Choice Awards on March 27, 2010.

season and was more popular than ever. In March, Demi even admitted she was now dating one of the Jonas Brothers. It was Joe. She told *Access Hollywood*, "He's my best friend and he is incredible. ... [a] complete gentleman [who] treats me to the most amazing places. He's perfect." It is unclear exactly when the pair officially began dating. Of course, Demi had been denying such rumors since the filming of the *Camp Rock* movie in 2007. Some have suggested that the two became a couple at the end of 2009, while they were filming *Camp Rock 2: The Final Jam*.

That new movie premiered on the Disney Channel in September. Eight million people tuned in, most of them kids ages six to fourteen. That made the movie the number one cable movie of the year. Demi even found her way onto a prime-time series for adults on ABC called *Grey's Anatomy*. She played the part of Haley May, a troubled teen suffering from schizophrenia, a mental illness. Critics gave Demi favorable reviews for her performance.

Personal Struggles

Though no one knew it at the time, Demi was going through some mental health struggles of her own. That became clear to almost everyone at the end of October while she was on tour with Jonas Brothers. During a flight to Peru, Demi went up to one of the Jonas Brothers' backup dancers, twenty-one-year-old Alex Welch, and punched her in the face. Pictures of Welch with a black eye soon surfaced online. People wondered why Demi would do such a thing. According to Welch, Demi believed she had tattled on her to tour managers for some things she had done while on a night out. Welch told the London *Daily Mail*, "We were on the plane with the Jonases having this awesome time and ... she walks up and punches me and literally walked away and got in her seat."

Demi later admitted what she had done. She told *Elle* magazine, "I just felt like she betrayed me. Right after, I texted my mom and just said, 'I'm sorry.'" Some said Demi lost it because she was upset over the fact that Joe Jonas, whom she had by that time broken up with, was now dating *Twilight* star Ashley Green. Another theory was that Demi was upset over the death of a friend. Demi said it wasn't just one thing. She said there were many things going on in her life that caused her meltdown.

Demi Lovato attends Z100's Jingle Ball '11 kick-off party at the Aeropostale Times Square store, in New York, on October 21, 2011.

The incident on the plane had a big impact on Demi's career and on her life. She immediately dropped out of the tour and checked into a treatment center in Illinois for emotional and physical issues. Exactly what those issues were wasn't specified. For a long time, there had been rumors floating around that Demi was a cutter, someone who intentionally cuts herself for psychological reasons. Close-up pictures of her wrists with what appeared to be scars on them from cutting surfaced on the Internet.

Shortly before she had to cut off her tour and seek treatment, Demi helped singer Taio Cruz announce the American Music Award nominations on October 18, 2012.

▲ On August 7, 2011, celebrity presenters Tyler Posey and Charice Pempengco gave Demi Lovato the Acuvue Inspire Award at the Teen Choice Awards. Lovato also won an award that night for her song "Skyscraper."

Demi later admitted she had been hurting herself in that way since she was eleven years old. She said on *Good Morning America*, "It was a way of expressing my own shame, of myself, on my own body. I was matching the inside to the outside. And there were some times where my emotions were just so built up, I didn't know what to do. The only way that I could get instant gratification was through an immediate release on myself." Demi also admitted she had developed an eating disorder when she was just eight years old. She said it began right around the time in elementary school where her jealous peers began calling her fat.

There were also rumors that Demi had entered treatment because she was addicted to drugs and alcohol. People close to her repeatedly said that was not the case. But two years later, Demi admitted she had gotten in trouble with them. She told *Seventeen* magazine she did those things to numb the emotional pain she felt inside. She said, "I'm not gonna lie. ... I was doing things like drinking and using [drugs]."

Demi spent three months in the treatment facility. While she was there she continued to reach out to her fans. She wrote on her Facebook page, "I want to make sure my fans know how thankful I am for all their love, support and prayers during this difficult time. Thank you for standing beside me through it all." When she left treatment, Demi paid tribute to those fans by getting a heart tattooed on her wrist. She said it was because a group of her fans drew hearts on their own wrists every day she was in treatment. It was their way of supporting her.

Demi attended the Camp Rock 2 premiere on August 18, 2010.

Demi said many celebrities, including Selena Gomez, Miley Cyrus, and Taylor Swift, reached out to her to give support when they found out she was in treatment.

While in treatment, Demi discovered she was bipolar. Those who are bipolar experience severe mood swings. Sometimes, they are super excited. Other times, they are super depressed. Demi said after she was diagnosed, her life up to that point suddenly made sense. She told *People* magazine, "I feel like I am in control now where my whole life I wasn't in control."

Demi decided not to go back to work on *Sonny with a Chance*. She felt being in front of the cameras would not be good for her and might make her too self-conscious. Demi instead focused on getting better and on her music career. She opened up to several members of the media about the difficulties she had faced. Her goal in doing so was to help others in similar situations. Also, talking about one's problems is an important part of the recovery process.

Inspiring Others

As a singer, Demi was also able to share her message through her songs. That's exactly what she did with *Unbroken*, her third album. Demi told *Seventeen* magazine, "It's been very therapeutic to be able to express my feelings and talk about who I really am, through my music. ... I'm hoping to provide inspiration for girls everywhere who are going through the same issues I've faced."

Unbroken was released in September 2011. The first single was "Skyscraper." Although she did not write it, Demi was excited to record the song, which she found inspirational. Its lyrics talked about overcoming obstacles, remaining strong, and "rising from the ground like a skyscraper." Demi told *Seventeen* the song was, "really special to me—to me it symbolizes my journey from the person I was to the happy healthy person I am today, and the fact that people are able to rise above anything, despite the odds."

Critics were impressed by "Skyscraper." The single reached number ten on the *Billboard* charts, and won a *Teen Choice* award for best summer song. Other songs on *Unbroken*, especially the ones co-written by Demi, were personal, too. The most personal was "For the Love of a Daughter." In it, Demi sings about her estranged relationship with her birth father, talking about how long it had been since they had last spoken and how he had manipulated her so many times that even when he told her he loved her she did not believe him. Demi told the *New York Daily News* she had to cut off all connection with her father. "It was hurting me too much," she said.

▲ Demi Lovato (right) and Wilmer Valderrama (left) join actress Rosario Dawson as they wait to record a public service announcement for Latino voting rights. Some people thought Lovato had dated the much-older Valderrama.

The song became the most recent chapter in what had been a difficult history between father and daughter. When Demi was in treatment, Patrick Lovato had been criticized by family members for saying he feared something like that might happen to his daughter when she first signed with Disney.

41

At the end of 2011, Patrick Lovato once again tried to get Demi to talk to him, telling *RadarOnline* that he had cancer and wanted to see her and her sister, Dallas. He said, "My health isn't what it used to be and I know my daughter loves her daddy, so please call me Demi." If Demi ever did call her father, it was not reported in the media.

Near the end of 2011, Demi's relationship with actor Wilmer Valderrama began making tabloid headlines. The relationship had begun when Demi was eighteen years old and Valderrama was thirty. It was believed that the pair ultimately broke up because of their big age difference. Demi had also been linked to an even older man, actor Ryan Phillippe. Phillippe was a thirty-six-year-old divorced father when the two allegedly dated in mid-2011. Demi was eighteen then, too.

In December, Demi lashed out at the company that made her career, the Disney Channel. She felt one female character's lines in the series *Shake It Up* had made fun of eating disorders. The character said, "You're adorable. I could just eat you guys up. You know … if I ate." Demi went on Twitter to share her thoughts: "I find it really funny how a company can lose one of their actress' from the pressures of an EATING DISORDER and yet still make jokes about that very disease." She later tweeted: "Dear Disney Channel, EATING DISORDERS ARE NOT SOMETHING TO JOKE ABOUT." Demi's popularity spurred Disney to action. The channel responded immediately and took the offending episode off the air.

Staying Strong

In March 2012, Demi was featured on an MTV special program called *Demi Lovato: Stay Strong*. Exactly what the program was about was kept secret up until airtime. "Stay" and "Strong" were the two words Demi had tattooed on the inside of her wrists, along with the heart for her fans, shortly after she left rehab. Her fans wondered: Could that be some sort of clue?

As it turns out, it was. The show was about Demi's vow to "stay strong" in the face of what she said was going to be a long road to getting healthy. She even admitted that she had continued to harm herself after she was released from treatment. She said, "I can not tell you that I have not thrown up since treatment [due to her eating disorder]. I can not tell you that I have not cut myself since treatment. I'm not perfect."

Demi suffered from bulimia, a form of eating disorder in which someone overeats, then forces herself to throw the food back up so she doesn't gain weight. Bulimia can severely harm various parts of the body, and can even be fatal if it isn't treated.

The special covered Demi's entire life. She talked about her time on *Barney & Friends*, when she felt inadequate because she

Demi Lovato at an appearance for Z100 fans at the iHeartRadio Theater in New York City.

was a bit pudgy and her friends were the "young kids that had flat stomachs." She talked about her life growing up in Texas, and said the whole time she lived there she was unhappy and sick. She said, "I had a good childhood, but there were things that definitely interrupted it. I battled depression at a really young age which started when I was seven years old."

She even talked about how the fame she had obtained during her *Camp Rock* days affected her mental health: "Everyone kind of just made me a role model and I hated that. I was partying, I was self-medicating. I was like, 'Why would you want your kids to be like me?' I felt like I was living a lie. I was dealing with all this pain emotionally and I felt guilt and shame."

Demi Lovato performing during her summer concert tour at the Greek Theatre in Los Angeles in 2012.

Demi Lovato attends the ▶
*The X Factor season finale
results show in Los Angeles
in December, 2012.*

Demi even talked about
her future during the MTV
special, and the difficulties
she knows lie ahead. She said,
"This is a daily battle that I
will face the rest of my life."

The morning before *Stay
Strong* aired, Demi woke
early and went on the *Today
Show*. She sang her latest
hit single, "Give Your Heart
a Break," live on national
TV. Before she sang she
talked about her life, the
upcoming *Stay Strong*
special, and what she feels
is her purpose in life. Demi
said, "I've decided to tell
my story because there are
a lot of young teens, girls and boys, that are dealing with the
same issues that I've been through. If I'm able to use my voice
to do good in the world then I definitely want to do that."

Further Info

Books

Edwards, Posy. *Demi Lovato: Star of Camp Rock*. London, England: Orion, 2008.

Meinking, Mary. *Demi Lovato*. North Mankato, MN: Capstone Press, 2013.

Rajczak, Kristen. *Demi Lovato*. New York: Gareth Stevens Pub., 2012.

Rutherford, Lucy. *Demi Lovato and Selena Gomez: The Complete Unofficial Story of the BFFs*. Toronto: ECW Press, 2009.

Tracy, Kathleen. *Demi Lovato*. Hockessin, Del.: Mitchell Lane Publishers, 2010.

Internet Addresses

Demi's official Web site
www.demilovato.com

Demi's official Facebook page
www.facebook.com/demilovato

Demi's official YouTube page
www.youtube.com/user/therealdemilovato

Index

A

acting career
  Barney & Friends,
    11–14
  As the Bell Rings, 18–19
  Camp Rock, 19–23, 29
  *Camp Rock 2: The Final
    Jam*, 30, 32
  casting calls, 11–12,
    16, 17
  guest roles, 14, 16, 32
  *Princess Protection
    Program*, 27, 28
  Sonny with a Chance,
    19, 26–27, 35

B

bullying, 15, 24

C

charity work, 23–24
Cutler, Scott, 28
Cyrus, Miley, 17, 23, 39

D

De La Garza, Madison, 14
De La Garza Eddie,
  9–10, 20
Demi Lovato: Stay Strong,
  43–44, 46
Disney Channel, 16–19,
  26, 42

E

eating disorders, 37,
  42

F

"For the Love of a
  Daughter," 40

G

Gomez, Selena, 11–12,
  14–19, 23, 27, 39

H

Hannah Montana, 17, 26
homeschooling, 15–16

J

Jonas, Joe, 20, 22, 25–26,
  30, 33
Jonas Brothers, 20,
  23–26, 28, 31–33

L

Linley, Cody, 26
Lovatics, 6–8, 34
Lovato, Dallas, 9, 10,
  14, 37
Lovato, Demi
  birth, 9
  childhood, family life,
    9–10, 14, 22–23
  education, 14–16, 28
  social life, 25–26, 30,
    42
Lovato, Dianna, 9, 14, 16
Lovato, Patrick, 9, 22–23,
  40, 42

M

mental health issues
  bipolar disorder, 39
  bulimia, 37
  cutting, 35, 39
  exhaustion, 29
  meltdown, 33, 35
  substance abuse, 37
  treatment, 35, 37, 39
  triumph, 6–7
"Moves Me," 15

S

singing career
  auditions, 19
  concert tours, 23–24,
    28, 33
  Don't Forget, 24–25
  Here We Go Again, 28
  inspiration for, 39–40,
    43–44, 46
  lessons, 10, 14
  songwriting, 14–15,
    24–25
  talent shows, 10
  Unbroken, 39–40
"Skyscraper," 39–40
Swift, Taylor, 39

T

Teen Choice Award, 40

V

Valderrama, Wilmer, 42

W

Welch, Alex, 33
World Series 2011, 5–8